DK

LIFE Stories

QUEEN ELIZABETH

DK LIFE Stories

QUEEN ELIZABETH II

by Brenda and Brian Williams

Illustrated by Charlotte Ager

Senior Editor Marie Greenwood
Project Editor Kritika Gupta
Editorial Assistants Abi Luscombe, Kieran Jones
Senior Art Editor Ann Cannings
Project Art Editors Roohi Rais, Lucy Sims
Assistant Art Editor Simran Lakhiani
US Senior Editor Shannon Beatty
Jacket Coordinator Issy Walsh
Jacket Designers Dheeraj Arora, Brandie Tully-Scott
Jacket Illustrator Alessandra de Cristofaro
DTP Designers Sachin Gupta, Vijay Kandwal
Project Picture Researcher Sakshi Saluja
Production Editor Dragana Puvacic
Production Controller John Casey
Managing Editors Jonathan Melmoth, Monica Saigal
Managing Art Editors Diane Peyton Jones, Ivy Sengupta
Delhi Team Head Malavika Talukder
Creative Director Helen Senior
Publishing Director Sarah Larter
Subject Consultant Dr. Elena Woodacre
Literacy Consultant Stephanie Laird

This American Edition, 2023
First American Edition, 2020
Published in the United States by DK Publishing
1745 Broadway, 20th Floor, New York, NY 10019

A catalog record for this book
is available from the Library of Congress.
ISBN: 978-0-7440-8911-0 (Paperback)
ISBN: 978-0-7440-8912-7 (Hardcover)

DK books are available at special discounts when purchased
in bulk for sales promotions, premiums, fund-raising, or educational use.
For details, contact: DK Publishing Special Markets,
1745 Broadway, 20th Floor, New York, NY 10019
SpecialSales@dk.com

Printed and bound in China

For the curious
www.dk.com

Dear Reader,

Elizabeth II reigned for longer than any other queen in world history. In the UK, Queen Victoria's reign had lasted for 63 years and 216 days. Elizabeth broke her great-great-grandmother's record on September 9, 2015.

Elizabeth never expected to be queen—she only became next in line to the throne when a twist of fate made her father the king. She grew up during World War II, married and had children. Royal life was briefly normal. With the death of her father, all changed again. Elizabeth was queen, and had a duty for life.

Being queen meant being on public show. Although the Queen had no real power, and did not vote, she had endless government business to read, and she signed off each new law. She traveled the world and was photographed perhaps more than anyone else. Yet the woman behind this royal image was seen by very few. Elizabeth had promised that her life would be one of service and she dedicated her life to doing her duty. In this she never wavered—an example to all.

Happy reading,
Brenda and Brian Williams

The life of...
Queen
Elizabeth II

Chapter 1

Royal baby

On April 21, 1926, Number 17 Bruton Street in the fashionable district of Mayfair, London, was unusually full of people.

Elizabeth, the Duchess of York, was about to give birth to her first baby, and her husband, Albert, had "first baby" nerves. As well as doctors, nurses, and servants, a government minister—the Home Secretary—was present. For this was no ordinary birth—Albert was the

Duke of York, one of the sons of King George V of the United Kingdom (UK). The young duchess was glad to have an old friend with her—Clara Knight, who cared for the children. She had worked for the family since Elizabeth was a young girl.

Elizabeth had married Albert—known as Bertie—in 1923. Since then, the couple had lived a fairly quiet life. Bertie was shy and had a stammer, which meant he could not always talk smoothly and fluently. It was his elder brother Edward who took the headlines. Edward was the Prince of Wales and also the heir to the throne. He was stylish and popular—a modern prince who many thought would one day be a modern king.

The Prince of Wales enjoyed public life. Here he is in Australia in 1920.

Bertie in Royal Air Force (RAF) uniform

Bertie was not particularly stylish, and did not like being on show. He had been an officer on a navy battleship, and was the first British royal to pilot a plane. However, he hated making speeches and was nervous around his gruff father. Duchess Elizabeth, on the other hand, could make King George laugh. She said "His Majesty" could, when he chose, be very funny, too. Elizabeth's easy ways and natural charm offered valuable support to her husband. They enjoyed some official duties, such as watching RAF displays together in London.

The young couple didn't have their own home yet, which was why their first baby was born at 17 Bruton Street, which belonged to Elizabeth's parents. Home births were not unusual in the 1920s, but this one had a slight problem. Luckily, the doctors were able to perform an operation called a Caesarean section. All went well, and at 2:40 a.m., to the parents' great delight, a baby girl was born. The Home Secretary informed the Lord Mayor of London, and the palace official woke King George V and Queen Mary at 4 a.m. to tell them of their grandchild's arrival. "Such a relief and joy," the Queen wrote in her diary.

DID YOU KNOW?

By law, a government minister had to check royal births in case an "outsider" baby was smuggled in.

What is a Caesarean section? An operation to help a mother give birth. It's also called a C-section.

The morning papers reported the birth, of course, but their headlines were also full of scary warnings of a nationwide "general strike." The shutdown began on May 3, 1926, halting trains and buses, and bringing mines and factories to a standstill.

On May 29, baby Elizabeth Alexandra Mary was christened in the chapel at Buckingham Palace. The baby wore the same lace gown made for Queen Victoria's children, and was baptized at a font filled with water from the River Jordan (the river in which Jesus was baptized, according to the Bible). Baby Elizabeth cried the whole time.

GENERAL STRIKE

A general strike is when most workers in a country refuse to work. The 1926 General Strike was the first time this had happened in the UK. It was only eight years after the end of World War I, and times were hard. The UK's mines produced coal for factories, trains, and homes. When mine-owners tried to cut their pay, miners stopped work in protest. Other workers joined them, but the strike lasted only nine days, before people returned to work.

QUEEN VICTORIA

Princess Elizabeth was Queen Victoria's great-great-granddaughter. Victoria came to the throne in 1837, at just 18 years old, and she died in 1901. She had reigned longer than any previous king or queen in Britain's history. Through many royal marriages, her family had spread across Europe, so baby Elizabeth had royal relatives in lots of countries.

The King had thought about naming his granddaughter Victoria, but decided not to, since the little princess was unlikely ever to be queen. After all, he thought, his son and heir Edward would surely marry and have a child who would then be next in line to the throne. In any case, Bertie might also have more children, and any sons would automatically be placed ahead of Elizabeth, since she was a girl.

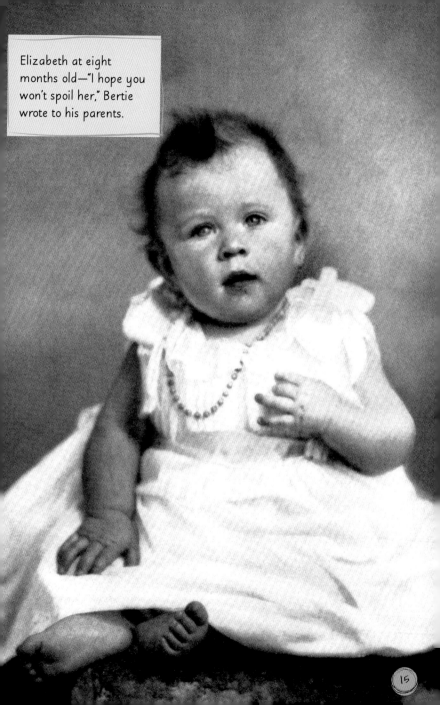

Elizabeth at eight months old—"I hope you won't spoil her," Bertie wrote to his parents.

Chapter 2

The LITTLE princess

Life for a royal baby was not the same as in most families. The princess was cared for mainly by nursery staff, led by Clara Knight.

Clara Knight was a farmer's daughter who became a nanny for the family. Though not married, she was always called Mrs. Knight by grown-ups and "Alla" by the children she took care of. The Duchess trusted Nanny Alla to look after baby Elizabeth. Women in high society, like the Duchess, did not spend all day, every day, with small children, no matter how much they loved them. In those days, the nanny was in charge. Nanny Alla made strict rules for the young Elizabeth to follow.

What is a nanny?

A nanny is someone who is paid to look after young children, and who sometimes lives with the family.

She made sure that Elizabeth was fed, bathed, dressed, and taken out in her stroller for fresh air, usually in nearby Berkeley Square. At playtime, the princess was only allowed one toy at a time, and when Elizabeth was old enough, she had to learn to put each toy away in its correct place. Mrs. Knight's helpers were Margaret MacDonald ("Bobo") and Bobo's sister, Ruby. Wherever the baby went, so did they, and the four of them spent many happy months together.

Clara Knight

All too soon, however, royal duty called. In January 1927, Elizabeth's parents set out for an official visit to Australia, leaving their baby at home. In an age before jet travel, their only option was a long, slow voyage by sea.

BRITAIN'S EMPIRE

King George V was officially a king-emperor, of the UK and the British Empire. In 1922, when the British Empire was at its peak, it covered about one-quarter of the world's land, with over 400 million people. It included Australia, New Zealand, South Africa, and Canada, which were self-governing, and India, which became independent in 1947, as well as many smaller lands. Queen Mary, Elizabeth's grandmother, gave the child wooden building blocks made from trees grown across this vast empire, as a present for her fourth birthday.

Elizabeth's parents would be away for six months. For Bertie, partly because of his stammer, the tour was a worrying ordeal of one public appearance after another. However, training by speech expert Lionel Logue gave him more confidence in speaking to an audience.

Lionel Logue

Baby Elizabeth stayed first in her grandparents' home in the countryside and then at Buckingham Palace, where King George was once again delighted to see his "sweet little grandchild." She soon had a pet name, Lilibet, which stuck within the family. She took her first steps, and her grandmother, Queen Mary, sent photos and letters to Australia, reporting that Lilibet had four teeth and was "quite happy." More good news followed soon—the new London home was now redecorated and ready for the family to move into. Photos of "the world's best-known baby" filled Australia's newspapers, and many people sent her presents. When the Duke and Duchess returned in June 1927, they brought back lots and lots of toys, including a Noah's Ark with kangaroos, koalas, and other Australian animals. Cheering Londoners greeted them as they stood waving on the balcony of their new house, 145 Piccadilly, London. It was the first time Lilibet had seen such a crowd, but it would not be the last.

A Guardsman on duty

The family's new home had servants to run it, a garden, and it was just a short walk from Buckingham Palace. The Duchess read her daughter stories and nursery rhymes, as did Nanny Alla. Elizabeth learned new rules— she must not walk back and forth in front of a soldier on guard at the Palace. If she did, he would have to "present arms" (hold up his rifle to salute her). This was not fair or kind, Elizabeth was told. Also, she was not to drop teddy bears on visitors from the top of the stairs!

Not long before her third birthday, little Elizabeth visited the coast at Bognor in Sussex, where "Grandpa England" was recovering from illness. Just watching his granddaughter playing in the sandbox helped make King George feel better.

Princess Elizabeth helps hold sister Margaret still for a photo with their mother, the Duchess of York.

The Duchess of York holds her new baby, Margaret Rose.

The princesses arrive with Nann Alla for their vacation in Scotlan

Swimming at the beach was out of the question—after all, this little girl was a princess. However, Elizabeth was about to get a pet, and later a playmate.

For her fourth birthday, in April 1930, the King gave her a Shetland pony, which was named Peggy. Then later in the year, Elizabeth got a baby sister, born on August 21. She was given the name Margaret Rose, but Elizabeth said she was going to call her "Bud." When asked why, she replied: "Well, she's not a real Rose yet, is she? She's only a bud." Alla now took charge of the baby, while Bobo took care of Elizabeth. Afterward, Bobo rarely left her side, remaining a loyal friend until she died at the age of 89.

Chapter 3

Royal sisters

The two sisters played and learned together as the world moved on around them. But little could Elizabeth have imagined what lay ahead...

Margaret was a lively prankster, full of fun. Elizabeth was quieter, sensible, and protective of her younger sister. She rarely lost her temper and seemed to understand what being a princess meant. It meant "duty." King George, supposedly a rather stern man, was devoted to his granddaughters. Servants were once startled to see the King playing with the children on the floor, being led along by his beard!

From 1932, Elizabeth's family had a weekend country house in Windsor Great Park, given to them by the King. It had large gardens, just the place for children to climb, dig, and get muddy. There was a new garden playhouse too, Y Bwthyn Bach ("The Little House"), a present from the people of Wales. Here, the girls could make dinner for their parents, since everything in the play house worked—lights, water, stove—even if the grown-ups had to stoop to get in.

Elizabeth and Margaret also had lessons together, not at school, but at home with a governess. Her name was Marion Crawford (soon to be known as Crawfie). At age 23,

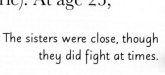

The sisters were close, though they did fight at times.

she was college-educated and interested in giving the princesses as "modern" a royal education as she could.

Most days the princesses spent a short time after breakfast with their parents, before lessons began in the classroom. Here, seated at desks, Miss Crawford was in charge of the girls each day from 9 a.m. In the morning there were regular lessons. After lunch came singing, music, and dancing. Sometimes there'd be an afternoon outing—perhaps to nearby Hamilton Gardens, where they could at least see other children, or a walk in Green Park. Visits to Madame Tussaud's waxworks or London Zoo were special treats. So was a ride on the top deck of a red London bus, peering down at the busy city streets. Tea was at 4:45 p.m., with their parents. Sometimes, Elizabeth's uncle, Edward, Prince of

Elizabeth loved ponies, and most of all enjoyed going for rides with her father.

Wales, joined them. After tea, there were often card games, such as Snap. Bath time was followed by boisterous pillow fights with Mummy and Papa before bed. The princesses slept in a nursery at the very top of the house. Elizabeth kept her toy horses outside on the landing, putting them to bed each night. Elizabeth was a neat child, placing books in order on the shelf and folding her clothes at night. One Christmas, she even got a dustpan and broom as a present!

The Duke was very proud of his children. He praised Elizabeth's drawing when she made cards for family birthdays and listened to the girls playing the piano. (Margaret was the more musical one). While the Duchess read bedtime stories such as *Black Beauty*, Queen Mary made sure the girls also read

Elizabeth did her best to sit corgis Jane and Dookie for this photo.

books about history and the British Empire. The two girls spent many happy hours riding ponies and playing with their pet dogs. The first Welsh corgi pup joined the family in 1933. His name was Dookie, and he was the first of more than 30 royal corgis.

As a bridesmaid at her Uncle George's wedding, Elizabeth *(sitting, right)* had to hold the bride's train.

The girls spent most days together. They rarely played with friends their own age, though they did meet their cousins at Christmas parties and at family weddings.

In November 1934, Elizabeth, now eight years old, was bridesmaid at the wedding of her Uncle George, Duke of Kent, to Princess Marina of Greece and Denmark. Among the guests was a fair-haired teenage boy—a distant cousin whose name was Prince Philip of Greece. Elizabeth was finding out how large her royal family was.

In 1935, King George and Queen Mary celebrated 25 years on the throne. Flags were flown, bands played, and crowds cheered at the Jubilee parade from Buckingham Palace to St. Paul's Cathedral.

"I'M THREE, YOU ARE FOUR"

This is what Princess Elizabeth told her sister Princess Margaret when their grandfather George V died and their uncle became King Edward VIII. Edward had no children and so his younger brother Albert (Elizabeth's father) was his heir. Then came Elizabeth, and after her, Margaret.

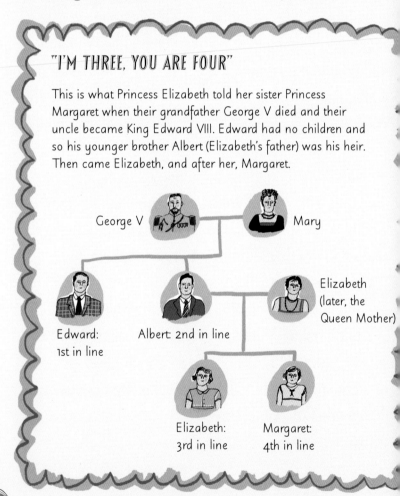

George V   Mary

Edward: Albert: 2nd in line   Elizabeth
1st in line   (later, the
                                                Queen Mother)

Elizabeth: Margaret:
3rd in line   4th in line

The princesses rode in the carriage procession, wearing pink dresses and straw hats. Yet the family was concerned, because when the King made his 1935 Christmas radio broadcast, he sounded very sick.

The Christmas vacation was spent at Sandringham in Norfolk, where Elizabeth walked with her grandfather on one of his last outings. On January 17, she returned home with her parents. That same day, the King, now kept in bed, wrote in his diary that he felt "rotten." Three days later, he died. News flashed around the world: "The King is dead … Long live the King." Elizabeth's uncle was the new king—King Edward VIII, and Elizabeth had moved up one place in the line to the throne.

31

Chapter 4

Destiny calls

Elizabeth's uncle—not yet crowned King Edward VIII—seemed carefree at first. But he was about to make an important decision …

In 1936, Edward told his family and friends that he wanted to marry his close companion, Wallis Simpson. Most people in Britain knew little about her, except that she was American—and a married woman.

Wallis set about getting a divorce. By May 1937, the date planned for the King's coronation, she would be free to marry him. This was a problem for the British Government and the Church of England. They had agreed that the King might marry, but had also said

---

What is a coronation?

A coronation is a religious ceremony to crown a new king or queen.

that his wife could never be "Queen Wallis." He must choose. Be king or marry Wallis—he could not do both.

As the arguments raged, life went on much as usual for Elizabeth. One thing she enjoyed was swimming, so she started lifeguard training. However, at the same time she could see how worried her father was about his older brother.

MRS. SIMPSON AND THE PRINCE

Wallis Simpson was raised in Baltimore, Maryland. After her first divorce in 1927, she married US-born, British shipowner Ernest Simpson. Wallis enjoyed London high society and in 1931 she met the Prince of Wales and they fell in love. She decided to divorce Ernest so that she could marry Edward. When he took Wallis to meet the York family in 1936, Elizabeth was curious.

Bertie himself wrote in his diary of the "awful and ghastly suspense" of the situation.

At last the new King made up his mind. If the woman he loved could not be queen, he would abdicate—meaning he would give up the throne forever.

On December 11, 1936, Edward VIII spoke on the radio to tell the world of his decision. "I have found it impossible … to discharge my duties as king as I would wish to do without the help and support of the woman I love," he said. From this moment on, Elizabeth's life changed forever. The next day, she saw a crowd outside her home. Someone shouted, "Long live King Albert!"

and she knew this meant her father. Her mother said sadly they would "have to make the best of it."

Elizabeth, in her calm and matter-of-fact way, sat down to make notes on her lifeguard training. She headed the page "Abdication Day." Later, seeing a letter addressed to "HM (Her Majesty) the Queen," she said, "That's Mummy now, isn't it?" When Elizabeth told Margaret that their father was king, Margaret asked, "Does that mean that you will have to be the next queen?" Elizabeth said it did. "Poor you," her sister replied.

Edward left Britain, and his family, at once. After marrying Wallis he lived abroad as the Duke of Windsor. Elizabeth's father chose not to keep his own name as king, but be called George VI. After Christmas, he moved with his family into Buckingham Palace. It was chilly in the

Buckingham Palace

palace, with many long staircases and corridors. Elizabeth even spotted mice. The garden was good to explore, though, with its trees and lake. It had a summerhouse, too, which made a perfect base for the Palace Girl Guides.

Elizabeth's father was crowned King on May 12, 1937. At 5 a.m., a band playing outside woke the princesses up. Elizabeth and Margaret dressed in purple velvet robes, with small crowns on their heads. Then came the carriage ride to Westminster Abbey, where kings and queens had been crowned for almost a thousand years.

THE PALACE GIRL GUIDES

The Girl Guides is the British version of the Girl Scouts, in which girls learn about outdoor skills and becoming a good citizen. At Buckingham Palace, a Girl Guides' group was formed for Elizabeth, and a Brownies' group for Margaret. They had meetings and learned new skills to earn badges.

On May 12, 1937, Elizabeth stood on the palace balcony with her parents, the newly crowned king and queen.

Elizabeth watched spellbound, feeling "a sort of haze of wonder as Papa was crowned." The coronation service was very long. Elizabeth made sure Margaret did not fidget too much: "I only had to nudge her once or twice ..." Though Elizabeth herself and "Grannie" (Queen Mary) did wonder how much longer the service would go on for. Afterward came the carriage ride, the balcony, photos, and then tea, and bed. Elizabeth fell asleep as soon as her head hit the pillow.

The princesses saw less of their father now, since he was very busy. There were weekends at Windsor, with the horseback rides Elizabeth loved, but important visitors came, too. This meant the sisters always had to be on their best behavior. At Buckingham Palace garden parties, Elizabeth grew more used to chatting with strangers. The King arranged extra lessons for her, in British history and government. This was to help her understand what it would mean to be queen.

In May 1939, the King and Queen visited the United States. President Roosevelt had invited

President Franklin
D. Roosevelt

the princesses along, but it was decided they were too young. While her parents were away, Elizabeth used a special camera to take photos and films to show them.

They replied with the first royal transatlantic phone call. Soon they were all home for the rest of the summer, and paid a visit to the King's old school, Dartmouth naval college. That day, Princess Elizabeth once again met her distant cousin Philip, now a naval cadet. He was 18, and less shy than she was. He made jokes and showed off by leaping over the net on the tennis court. He said he was looking forward to going to sea. He might have to fight too, since everyone said there could soon be a war …

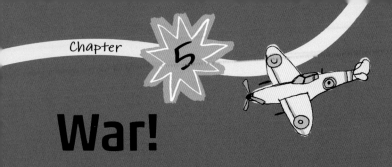

Chapter 5

War!

In September 1939, Elizabeth and Margaret were on vacation when grim news came on the radio—Britain was at war with Germany.

Their parents hurried back to London, leaving the girls at Balmoral Castle in Scotland with Nanny Alla, Bobo, and Miss Crawford. Elizabeth was just 13, and her history lessons now had to be sent to Balmoral by mail.

Christmas drew near, and life seemed almost normal. Elizabeth went shopping in Aberdeen for Christmas presents, before the family met again back at Sandringham in England for the festive holiday.

No bombing raids had yet hit British cities, but many children from London had already been evacuated to the countryside.

EVACUEES

Evacuees were moved or "evacuated" from cities to escape air raids. When the war began, 750,000 British children became evacuees. Some were sent abroad, but most went to live with host-families in the countryside. The evacuees in the picture are waiting for a train. They wore name labels, but the army hats were put on for the photo!

It was thought that the princesses might be safer in Canada, but their mother insisted they should all stay put. "The children won't leave without me; I won't leave without the King; and the King will never leave." When the princesses did move, it was to Windsor Castle.

Windsor Castle

In 1940, bombing raids on Britain began. Attacks during the Blitz came mainly at night and sent whole districts of London up in flames. Six bombs fell on Buckingham Palace on September 13, 1940, but the King and Queen were unhurt. At Windsor Castle, the princesses slept guarded by soldiers in a tower built in the 1400s. It was very cold. Two nights after moving in, an air raid siren woke up the girls. Elizabeth calmly began to dress, but Miss Crawford ran in, telling them there was no time. They must

What does "Blitz" mean?

Short for "blitzkrieg" (German for "lightning war"), the Blitz was what British people called the bombing attacks on their cities by German aircraft.

put coats over their night clothes and hurry down to the shelter. The castle's deep dungeon made a good emergency shelter. It was also dark and creepy, with beetles scuttling around the mattresses

DID YOU KNOW?

In 1940, some feared that the Nazis might try to kidnap the royal family. The King and his staff at Windsor took shooting lessons, just in case.

put down to sleep on. No wonder the girls stayed awake! By the light of flickering candles, they read or played games until the "all clear" sounded. Then they hurried back to their own beds. The castle dungeons held a few secret surprises, too. One day, the princesses peered inside some hat-boxes hidden safely in the dark. There, packed in old newspapers, shone the Crown Jewels.

Families gathered around their radios for news and entertainment during the war. Somebody at the BBC had the idea of asking Princess Elizabeth to speak on a popular children's show. That was how, on October 13, 1940, the princess broadcast to children all around the world. She ended with "Come on, Margaret," who then said "Goodnight, children." It was Elizabeth's first public speech.

Elizabeth first went through the radio speech with her mother, adding extra touches. She made the broadcast with Margaret from her home at Windsor Castle.

"I can **truthfully** say to you all that we **children** at home are full of **cheerfulness** and **courage.**"

Princess Elizabeth, BBC radio broadcast, 1940

At Christmas, the sisters starred in a pantomime, staged with children from a local school. Margaret played Cinderella, with Elizabeth as Prince Charming.

All the family came to watch these Christmas shows, including Philip. For some time the princess had been writing to him. Philip was now in the Royal Navy, full of fun and stories about adventures at sea. The King and Queen

WORLD WAR II

World War II began in 1939 after Nazi Germany invaded Poland and then seized much of Europe. Britain and its European Allies fought against Germany. War spread in 1941, when Japan attacked the United States at Pearl Harbor, and German armies invaded Russia. Armies, navies, and air forces fought across Europe, Asia, Africa, and the Pacific Ocean. Millions lost their lives, including six million Jews killed by the Nazis. Cities and homes were left in ruins. When the war ended in 1945, the United Nations was set up to help keep world peace.

liked him, but King George thought Elizabeth too young to fall in love.

Meanwhile, war continued to rage. In 1942, Elizabeth turned 16, the age at which young women had to sign up for war work. She wanted to do something practical, such as volunteer as a nurse in London, but the King said the city was too dangerous.

In October of that year, Mrs. Eleanor Roosevelt visited the UK and spent a night in Buckingham Palace. She slept in the Queen's bedroom, where bombs had shattered all of the windows. Mrs. Roosevelt also met the princess. She told the president that Elizabeth had "a great deal of character and personality."

Eleanor Roosevelt

The King was even less inclined to let his daughter do war work after his brother, the Duke of Kent, was killed in a military plane crash. Elizabeth had to wait—but she was still determined to do her part. Then in 1944, the princess joined the women's branch of the British Army. In the ATS (Auxiliary Territorial Service), she learned to drive and repair army trucks. The King was impressed to meet his grease-stained princess, who wasn't afraid of getting dirty. Like all ATS members, the princess was given a number and her details recorded: "Number 230873. Second Subaltern Elizabeth Alexandra Mary Windsor. Age 18. Eyes: blue. Hair: brown. Height: 5 ft 3 in."

That same year, Elizabeth made her first live speech in public, at a London children's hospital. Although still shy, she had grown into an impressive young lady.

War in Europe ended in May 1945. In London and other big cities, people partied to mark the Allies' victory. Elizabeth stood with her parents on the palace balcony, waving to the huge mass of people below. With them was Winston Churchill, who had led the British Government since 1940. That evening, the two princesses slipped out to join the crowds singing and dancing in the streets.

Changing a truck wheel was just one of the skills Elizabeth learned in the ATS.

Romance AND marriage

Life in Britain was still hard after the war. But a royal romance was about to bring a touch of sparkle to people's lives.

Years after the war ended, store windows still had little to show. There were shortages of many things and food was still being rationed. Everyone was tired of saving up coupons from ration books to buy what they needed. King George felt sympathy for the British people, who worried constantly about food, clothes, and keeping warm. But people learned to make do with little and find fun where they could.

The princesses found enjoyment in doing jigsaws with friends and dancing

What were ration coupons?

Everyone had ration books, with coupons (vouchers) that could be exchanged for food or clothing.

around to music on the radio. Elizabeth still liked country life best—she loved horses and her corgi Susan. Margaret was interested in music, theaters, and dances.

Princess Elizabeth now had her own rooms (or section) in Buckingham Palace, with Bobo and two assistants—known as ladies-in-waiting—and a wide circle of friends. One of her friends was Prince Philip, who was hoping to have a career in the Royal Navy.

PRINCE PHILIP

Philip was born on the Greek island of Corfu on June 10, 1921. However, he was taken as a baby to live with the rest of Greece's royal family in exile abroad. He was related to the Danish, Russian, German, and British royal families, and shared the same great-great-grandmother as Elizabeth—Queen Victoria.

In the summer of 1946, Philip visited Elizabeth often. Her grandmother, Queen Mary, told a friend that the princess had made up her mind. The young couple hoped to marry, but the King wanted Elizabeth to see more of the world first.

In 1947, a royal visit to South Africa was planned. It was Elizabeth's first trip abroad, and the royal "firm" (as the King called the royal family) traveled together. In sunny South Africa, the family missed the 1947 winter, which was one of the UK's coldest ever. Back in London, Philip sat in his overcoat by candlelight, because of power cuts caused by fuel shortages. Many others were doing the same. Three days before leaving for home, Elizabeth celebrated her 21st birthday. Speaking by radio to the Commonwealth, she promised to dedicate her life to the duties that lay before her. "I declare before you all that my whole life, whether it be long or short, shall be devoted to your service ..."

Princess Elizabeth poses for a 21st birthday photo during the royal tour of South Africa in 1947.

Elizabeth told a friend that when they got home, there would be something else to celebrate.

On June 8, 1947, the King and Queen announced that Elizabeth would marry Philip. It was big news. Magazines printed photos of the princess. Reporters told readers she loved horses, dogs, dancing, knitting, reading, and songs, especially those from the latest hit musical *Oklahoma*. Others wondered if the country could afford a royal wedding and who this foreign prince was. News stories explained how Elizabeth and Philip were both related to Queen Victoria.

The wedding was on November 20, 1947. There were a few family

panics. As Bobo helped Elizabeth with her wedding dress, the bride's bouquet was lost— and found in a kitchen cupboard. The jeweled tiara ("something borrowed" from her mother) snapped and had to be repaired. The pearl necklace gift from her parents had been packed off with other wedding presents. It had to be found before the bride set out for Westminster Abbey with her father in the Irish State Coach—a horse-drawn carriage made for Queen Victoria. Otherwise, this was a royal

wedding with no frills. There was no public holiday, but there was a splendid wedding cake—even though powdered sugar was still being rationed. The government let the princess have 100 extra ration coupons for her wedding clothes.

Afterward, the King wrote to his daughter. He had been "so proud and thrilled" he said. The King added that he knew he would always be able to rely on Elizabeth and Philip to help him in his work. There was more good news to come. In November 1948, Elizabeth gave birth to a baby boy named Charles.

The following year, Philip took command of the warship HMS *Magpie*, based at Malta in the Mediterranean Sea. For a short while, the princess enjoyed "normal" life as a Navy wife and mother.

There was another addition to their young family, when, in 1950, Elizabeth gave birth to a baby girl named Anne. Everyone was

FESTIVAL OF BRITAIN

The 1951 Festival of Britain was an exhibition that showed off British industry, arts, and science. New London attractions, such as the Royal Festival Hall, Dome of Discovery, Skylon, and Battersea Fun Fair, were all part of the Festival.

delighted, but there was sadness, too. The King's health was failing. Public events, such as the opening of the Festival of Britain exhibition on May 3, 1951, had become a strain. In October, Elizabeth left with Philip for a royal visit to Canada. On her first transatlantic flight, lasting over 16 hours, Princess Elizabeth had plenty of time to think about the future.

Philip and Elizabeth with their children, Charles and Anne.

Chapter 7

A **new reign**

Elizabeth settled into her dual roles as a wife and mother, but her father, the King, was very ill. Her life was about to change forever.

In 1951, the princess took the ailing King's place at the Trooping the Colour parade, riding on horseback. Though not yet at ease at formal events, she also hosted a dinner for the King of Norway (her great-uncle). Her father had planned to make a Commonwealth tour, but his doctors wanted it delayed. Elizabeth was

What is Trooping the Colour?

When guards march their regiment's flag ("color") past troops at the royal birthday parade in London.

told she might have to take on more public duties, and this meant Philip must leave the Royal Navy to accompany her.

Helen Lightbody

The princess began to see less of her two small children, Charles and Anne. Their strict Scottish nanny was Helen Lightbody (known as "No-Nonsense"), who was helped by Mabel Anderson. Yet, however busy she was, the princess always played with the children after breakfast and after tea, before putting them to bed. Overseas visits meant leaving them behind, which was hard, but Elizabeth accepted this as part of the job.

A tour to North America in October 1951 meant that Elizabeth missed her son's third birthday, but she treasured a birthday photo of Charles with his grandfather. King George was still not well enough for his planned tour to Australia and New Zealand, so Elizabeth went in his place.

On January 31, 1952, Elizabeth waved goodbye to her parents as she and Philip left London airport on the first stage of the long journey. This included a stopover in Kenya, and a chance to see African wildlife, a thrill for someone like Elizabeth who loved animals. The princess was eager to take good shots with her camera while staying at Treetops, a cabin in a giant fig tree beside a waterhole. Here, rhinos, antelope, baboons, and other animals came to drink. Visitors to Treetops had to climb ladders, and as she clambered up, everyone held their breath as an elephant came very close. High in the branches was a great spot for photos, and

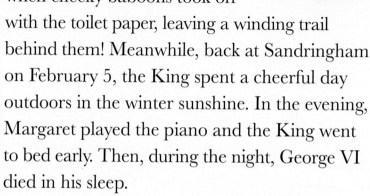

Elizabeth got busy with her camera. Everyone laughed when cheeky baboons took off with the toilet paper, leaving a winding trail behind them! Meanwhile, back at Sandringham on February 5, the King spent a cheerful day outdoors in the winter sunshine. In the evening, Margaret played the piano and the King went to bed early. Then, during the night, George VI died in his sleep.

In Kenya, Elizabeth's group was getting ready to leave when the sad news arrived from home. It was Philip who told her, as they walked in the garden. Elizabeth had always been very close to her father. He had tried to prepare her for this moment, when she would become queen. She had known, and thought about it, but the time had come far too soon. Elizabeth showed thoughtfulness toward the people with

DID YOU KNOW?

Elizabeth was told that an angry elephant could easily shake the branches in trees around Treetops. This meant the visitors' escape ladders were not totally safe!

her, saying she was sorry their trip was being cut short. She sent a message to her mother and got ready to go home. Philip was just as shocked, wondering what the future now held for him.

When asked what name she would use as queen, she answered, "My own name, Elizabeth, of course." Then came a short flight to Uganda's Entebbe airport, a delay caused by a thunderstorm, and a long flight to London. There were many hours to sit and think, before her plane landed on the evening of February 7. Churchill stood with government members, waiting. "Shall I go down alone?" she asked. In a black coat and hat, she stepped onto UK soil as the country's new sovereign.

The next day, she was formally proclaimed queen, promising to do her duty as her father had done.

Dressed in black in mourning for her father, Elizabeth left the plane to meet her government.

Even in such sadness, Elizabeth looked calm. She spoke clearly and listened carefully. When given official papers, she read them quickly, remembering everything. After all, she was to be queen not just of the UK, but of the entire Commonwealth.

After her father's funeral came plans for her coronation—and a new era. There was much to learn. Elizabeth was never late, never impatient, and did not appear to worry.

THE COMMONWEALTH

The Commonwealth is a group of nations that grew from the old British Empire. When Elizabeth became queen, the Commonwealth had 650 million people. Today, it has 2.4 billion citizens. Member states help each other through various organizations. Elizabeth valued being the symbolic head of this "family" of free nations. She visited almost all 56 Commonwealth countries and counted many of their leaders as friends.

Flag of the Commonwealth of Nations

There was plenty of time for planning, since the coronation was not to be held until June 2, 1953. As the day drew near, excitement grew. Soldiers were prepared for the ceremony and drilled to perfection. Uniforms and robes were brushed, buttons polished, horses groomed, and the coronation coach wheeled out for its first outing since 1937. Londoners put out flags, and people hung red, white, and blue buntings over houses and in streets across the country. People rushed to buy TV sets, since the coronation would be televised for the first time. This was a change the Queen had approved, when some had said TV cameras would intrude on the traditional ceremony. Elizabeth rehearsed very carefully what she would have to say and do. She even pinned sheets to her shoulders to practice walking with the coronation robe trailing behind her, and tried carrying weights on her head to get used to the heavy crown she would have to wear.

The day, when at last it arrived, was wet. Along the procession route thousands of people had sat all night under blankets to ensure they had a good view. Elizabeth wore a white satin gown, and rode in the Gold State Coach drawn by eight horses. Inside Westminster Abbey, she went through the three-hour ceremony without a stumble. She remembered that Queen Victoria had done this too, when Victoria was only 18. Serious and calm, the new Queen sat upright on the ancient oak coronation chair.

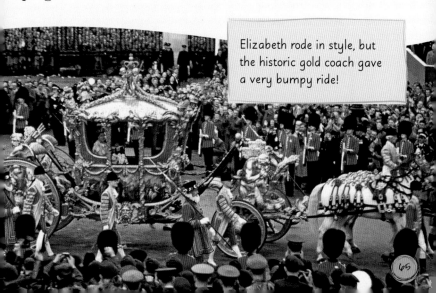

Elizabeth rode in style, but the historic gold coach gave a very bumpy ride!

THE CROWN JEWELS

The Crown Jewels are worn by British kings and queens at their coronations. These include St. Edward's Crown, a golden orb, long pole-like scepters, a ruby ring, swords, and spurs. Most were made for King Charles II in the 1660s. Monarchs can only wear St. Edward's Crown for coronations. They use the Imperial State Crown for all other events. The Imperial State Crown has over 2,800 diamonds, but is lighter than St. Edward's Crown.

One by one she took the emblems of state—spurs, sword, robe, ring, orb, scepters, and the crown. Her mother (now known as the Queen Mother) looked on, along with Elizabeth's young son, Prince Charles. He was sitting just as she had sat to see her father crowned.

Afterward, to the shouts of "God Save the Queen!", and thankful to be wearing the lighter Imperial State Crown, Elizabeth rode back through the crowds to stand on the palace balcony with her family. Newspapers spoke of "a new Elizabethan age," looking back to her ancestor Elizabeth I, who became queen in 1558 at the same age (25). It seemed a new era. What would it bring for the young Queen?

The crowned Queen,
holding the orb and
the scepter.

Chapter 8

Royal family ON view

On her travels around the globe, the Queen met world leaders, and while at home she busily carried out a long list of duties.

After the coronation in 1953 came a Commonwealth tour lasting five months. Elizabeth and Philip traveled more than 41,000 miles (66,000 km), visiting countries as large as Australia and as small as Tonga, an island in the South Pacific. With Elizabeth went her wedding dress, which she wore to open Australia's parliament. She told Australians that she would "not only rule but serve." However, looking happy all the time was hard. She wished she found it as natural as her mother, who was always smiling.

DID YOU KNOW?

On her 1953–54 tour, Elizabeth made 102 speeches and shook hands more than 13,000 times!

But she was still learning. Elizabeth had to concentrate, listen, and look the part. She knew that everyone she met would remember that time always.

Her tours had magic moments. In Tonga, for example, she met a tortoise left as a gift in the 1770s by the British explorer Captain Cook.

At home, Elizabeth's duties included weekly meetings with the Prime Minister. Her first prime minister was Winston Churchill, a trusted friend who was eager to give advice. Often their chats lasted 90 minutes or more, covering anything from atom bombs to horse racing.

WINSTON CHURCHILL

When Elizabeth was crowned, Winston Churchill was almost 80. He had led the UK during World War II, and yet he was nervous at first about working with a queen who, to him, seemed "a mere child." For her part, Elizabeth was in awe of the world-famous statesman, but they got along well. After Churchill retired in 1955, she missed their meetings. They were "always such fun" she said.

One discussion was more personal. Princess Margaret wanted to marry a former fighter pilot named Peter Townsend, who had been an equerry, or aide, to King George VI. But he was divorced, and had children. Churchill warned that Church and Commonwealth leaders would not approve. Elizabeth wanted her sister to be happy, but was concerned. After careful thought and taking advice from Elizabeth, Margaret decided not to marry Peter.

Elizabeth had two more children—Andrew in 1960 and Edward in 1964. Times started to

LOVE AND DUTY

Margaret met ex-Battle of Britain pilot Peter Townsend in 1944 when he joined King George VI's household staff. A royal princess needed permission to marry from the monarch, government, and Church of England. Peter was divorced, and the rules at the time meant that Margaret would have to give up her place in the royal line if she married him.

The Queen with Prince Andrew and the new baby in the family, Prince Edward.

change—new and exciting fashion, music, and ideas emerged in a period known as the "Swinging Sixties." Skirts were getting shorter and pop stars and groups, such as The Beatles and The Rolling Stones, attracted more interest than the royal family, which appeared boring and

BRITANNIA

This ship had a special place in the Queen's life. It was a "home from home," where the family could spend carefree days out of the public view when on tour around the world. *Britannia* was built in Scotland and was ready for service in 1954. It was a steamship fitted out as a home and office, but could also be turned into a floating hospital in time of war.

stuffy to some. There was a wedding too. Margaret had met someone new—society photographer Antony Armstrong-Jones. They married in 1960 and sailed away on honeymoon aboard the royal yacht *Britannia*. Having agreed with her dress designer that miniskirts were not for her, Elizabeth still knew the royal family must move with the times. She decided her children would go to school, rather than be taught at home, as she and her sister had been. So Prince Charles went to his father's old school in Scotland, and later attended Cambridge University. It was then time to make him Prince of Wales—a title held by the monarch's eldest son. Charles's investiture ceremony took place in Wales in 1969.

Elizabeth made her son Prince of Wales at Caernarvon Castle.

INVESTITURES

At investiture ceremonies, the Queen honoured people for outstanding achievements, whether in public service, the arts, sports, or other fields. Some awards are for bravery in everyday life or in war. When the Queen made a man a knight, she touched him lightly on each shoulder with a sword. This ancient ceremony of knighthood is called "dubbing." Women honored with a damehood become dames, but no sword is used.

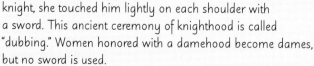

Never before had TV cameras shown the royal family at home, trying to look relaxed.

Elizabeth also decided to open part of Buckingham Palace as the Queen's Gallery, to show art from the royal collection. The Palace was reaching out, and the media lapped it up. It wanted more.

When growing up, Elizabeth had been seen by few outside her family. But now there was a TV in every home. Cameras followed her every move. The public was desperate to see what royal life was really like—and the Queen knew it was time to let them. First she allowed TV cameras into the royal palaces, to show some of their treasures. In 1969, she agreed to her family being filmed for a TV documentary called *Royal Family*. Not all her advisers thought this wise. People were worried that it might destroy some of the mystery around royalty. *Royal Family* gave TV viewers an inside look at many events, from the Queen talking with American President Richard Nixon to taking trips in her car, and buying ice cream. These snapshots of her life gave some glimpses of Elizabeth's quick sense of humor and fun, her skill as a mimic, and how hard she sometimes found it to keep a straight face.

9

Modern majesty

Queen Elizabeth had to learn to adapt to a changing world. But with new ideas and advances in technology came new dangers.

Elizabeth's full calendar led her to meet many world leaders, and some she grew to know very well. People were surprised by how easily she got along with politicians, even those known to be against the whole idea of monarchy. Life was changing, with less respect shown to powerful people and traditional ways of doing things. In newspapers or magazines, Elizabeth might see cartoons making fun of the royal

family or read articles asking if the monarchy should continue. Some thought it too costly, others claimed it earned the UK money by providing an

Chatting with Harold Wilson, Britain's Prime Minister from 1964–70 and from 1974–76.

added attraction for tourists to visit the country. The Commonwealth also seemed to matter less, with the UK now in the EEC (European Economic Community), which later became the European Union (EU).

The Queen never gave her opinion on politics and treated all sides with the same politeness. She found Harold Wilson, the Labour Prime Minister, easy to get along with. He came to Balmoral in 1976 with his wife, Mary,

What is the European Union?

A group of European countries that have close trade and other links. The UK left the EU in 2020.

to tell Elizabeth he was retiring, and she gave a cozy farewell tea. Afterward, she washed the dishes with Mary. They all knew the Queen would never retire. Her role was for life.

In the 1950s, the Queen and Prince Philip had enjoyed nights out together "undercover," at the movies or theater. By the 1970s, however, this was more difficult, since the Queen's safety became a big concern. As always, she had a police protection officer with her, but the threat was now not just from press cameras. Attacks from the IRA (Irish Republican Army) took place in Britain as a result of The Troubles.

THE TROUBLES

This was a conflict in Northern Ireland in the late 20th century. In 1921, Ireland had been split into the Irish Republic and Northern Ireland. Nationalists, who were mainly Catholic, wanted the island united. In Northern Ireland, most Protestants wanted to stay in the UK, and the Catholic minority faced discrimination. Violence from both sides broke out in Northern Ireland. Terrorism spread to British cities, with IRA bombings.

Aware of dangers, on and off duty, the Queen knew her every move was watched. Naturally shy, this made her more wary.

At home, with people she knew well, she could be herself. She could tell funny stories  about things going wrong on her visits, such as a hat blowing off, a flower bouquet dropped, or a driver getting lost. Philip could be impatient, and although Elizabeth too had a temper, she seldom lost it. People found her kind and understanding, and it was known that she could find it hard to say "no."

However, it was in the countryside that Elizabeth was at her most relaxed. Now a racehorse owner as well as a rider, she could often be found at the stables tending her horses. She read the racing news closely, along with the daily papers.

ALL THE QUEEN'S HORSES

Elizabeth adored horses from the age of four, when she first sat on Peggy the pony. She loved seeing her racehorses run, especially Aureole in the 1950s, Highclere in the 1970s, and Estimate, winner of the Ascot Gold Cup in 2013. She loved show-jumping too, proudly watching Princess Anne ride her horse Doublet to become European eventing champion of 1971. The Queen was particularly fond of riding her own Betsy, bought from a farmer, and Sanction, who seemed to understand her perfectly.

By 1977, Elizabeth had been queen for 25 years, but no one was sure how much enthusiasm her Silver Jubilee would generate. As ever, the government wanted to keep costs down, and so did she.

On tour, the Queen had a warm welcome in Australia, New Zealand, and the Pacific. When she came home, the celebrations in the UK took the government by surprise. Towns and villages organized street parties. A vast number of people (said to be a million) packed a road called the Mall in London to cheer the Queen as she drove to a church service

In towns and villages accross the country, people held street parties to celebrate the 1977 Silver Jubilee.

at St. Paul's Cathedral. Elizabeth lit a giant bonfire near Windsor Castle, the first of 100 other beacons to blaze across her realm.

That year, she also visited the Caribbean and Canada. She toured many parts of the UK, including Northern Ireland, where people were still living with the threat of violence from both sides in The Troubles.

Chapter 10

Ups AND downs

Elizabeth was happy to share her royal duties with her family. However, security issues and huge media attention created concern.

By the 1980s, the Queen was a grandmother and was as busy as ever. Elizabeth met people by the thousands, attending up to 400 engagements a year. She visited hospitals, disaster areas, churches, and grand balls. She had meetings with the UK's first female Prime Minister, Margaret Thatcher. She gave American President Ronald Reagan and Russian leader Mikhail Gorbachev the

In 1983, Ronald and Nancy Reagan were guests of the Queen and Prince Philip.

pomp and ceremony of state banquets. With Prince Philip by her side, she traveled the world for Commonwealth meetings, and the four-yearly Commonwealth Games. Every November, she laid the first poppy wreath at the Cenotaph in London.

What is the Cenotaph?   A London monument to honor those killed in war. "Cenotaph" means empty tomb.

PREPARING A ROYAL BANQUET

As head of state, the Queen hosted official dinners for foreign leaders at state banquets. Each one took weeks to prepare. Most state dinners were held at Buckingham Palace or Windsor Castle and everything had to be just right for the 150–160 guests. Staff made sure each seat, glass, plate, and knife, fork, and spoon were in the right place. Setting the table could take up to five days!

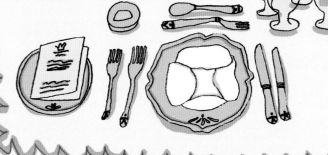

Living a private life was difficult, especially with the fear of terrorist attacks. Police protected the Queen day and night, but there were scares. On June 13, 1981, crowds cheered for Elizabeth at the Trooping the Colour parade. She was riding her trusted horse Burmese. Suddenly, shots rang out. Startled, the horse skittered. The Queen used all her skill as a horsewoman to stay in the saddle and

DID YOU KNOW?

Queen Elizabeth rode her faithful horse Burmese in 18 of her "official birthday" parades, from 1969 to 1986.

calm Burmese down as Life Guard troops galloped up to protect her. Fortunately, no one was hurt. The man the police arrested had fired blanks, which are not real bullets, though they make the same noise. Cool as ever, the Queen steadied Burmese, and they rode on.

Elizabeth had family concerns, too. Her eldest son, Prince Charles, was now in his 30s and not yet married. As heir to the throne, wasn't it time he settled down? Newspapers linked Charles with several girlfriends singling out Lady Diana Spencer. Her family and the Queen's knew each other well. Diana was just 20, shy, and seemed very happy to be engaged to the Prince.

Charles and Diana, after their engagement was announced.

85

Diana was big news and the public loved her. Diana was different. She acted more naturally, and seemed less stuffy than older royals. People found her warm and caring.

To the public's great delight the couple married in St. Paul's Cathedral, London, on July 29, 1981, before a vast TV audience.

Charles and Diana soon had a family of their own—William was born in 1982, and Henry (Harry) two years later. By now, the princess was a world celebrity, her picture on every front page. Her photos sold magazines, and paparazzi followed her everywhere. However, in private, Diana became unhappy. She found being part of the royal family a strain. Charles and Diana grew apart.

The Queen had challenges of her own. Buckingham Palace is guarded by police and soldiers, but in July 1982 its high walls failed

---

What are paparazzi?

Photographers who chase after celebrities and other famous people to get a photograph.

After the royal wedding in 1981, Diana took her place on the Palace balcony in front of the crowds and cameras.

Four generations of the royal family: the Queen Mother, the Queen with Prince William, Princess Diana holding baby Harry, and Prince Charles.

to keep out an unwelcome visitor. One morning, Elizabeth woke to find a man in her bedroom, opening the curtains. Although alarmed, the Queen kept her cool. She listened as the man sat on her bed talking of his family problems. Quietly, Elizabeth pushed her alarm button to call for help … but no one came. A maid was cleaning next door, the footman had taken the corgis for their walk, and the guard outside her room had gone off duty. Palace police heard the alarm and thought it was a mistake. When the man asked for cigarettes, Elizabeth said she would find some and left the room. She came back with the maid, footman, and dogs—and at last the police arrived. After an inquiry into this troubling incident, the Palace was made more secure.

Prince Andrew and Sarah on their wedding day.

Thankfully, there were happier times ahead. In 1986, Elizabeth's second son, Prince Andrew, married Sarah Ferguson. "Fergie" was fun and popular with the public, and the Queen made the couple the Duke and Duchess of York.

Elizabeth continued to follow her own interests, particularly her love of horses. She attended horse races with her mother and she enjoyed watching her daughter, Princess Anne, ride in show-jumping events.

Most of all, the Queen loved spending time relaxing with her ever-growing family, but little could she guess what lay ahead.

Troubled times

As the royal family grew, so did its problems. Elizabeth stayed as resolute as ever in the face of mounting pressures.

Elizabeth was to look back on 1992 as a particularly "horrible year." Her children's marriages were not proving as happy as she had hoped. Then in November, parts of Windsor Castle burned down. The fire, in a home with happy memories, left her sad and shocked.

Change was everywhere. The UK was

now part of the growing European Union, and from 1994 was linked to mainland Europe by the Channel Tunnel.

"1992 is not a year on which I shall look back with undiluted pleasure."

Queen Elizabeth II

91

MEETING MANDELA

The Queen was glad to see South Africa rejoin the Commonwealth in 1994 after the Apartheid years of white-only rule. On a visit in 1995, she met the country's new president, Nelson Mandela, freed after years in prison. He made a state visit to the UK a year later and returned in 2008 when he was 90. The Queen phoned him with birthday greetings, a sign of their easy friendship.

The Commonwealth was also changing. Elizabeth visited South Africa for the first time since 1947 and met Nelson Mandela. Two years later, she was in India and Pakistan to mark 50 years since the end of British rule. The two countries were now republics.

Tony Blair

Elizabeth celebrated her 70th birthday in 1996 and a year later gained a new prime minister, Tony Blair. People began talking about a younger "cool Britannia" in which the monarchy seemed old-fashioned. Some argued that Britain should become a republic with a president, similar to France or the United States. Newspapers in Canada called Elizabeth "boring." Australia chose a new national anthem to replace "God Save the Queen." The Queen could never answer back, of course, even when people were rude about her and her family. Instead, she took note of the criticism and made changes.

In 1997, the Queen and Prince Philip celebrated their golden wedding anniversary. Prince Philip praised her forbearance. She thanked him as her "strength and stay all these years."

Not all royal partnerships stood the test of time, however. August 1996 had marked the end of the fairy tale, with the divorce of Prince Charles and Princess Diana. Their private lives were private no longer. Books, TV interviews, news stories, and radio shows talked about them in ways unheard of when the Queen was young.

Queen Elizabeth was in Scotland when, early on August 31, 1997, news broke of Diana's death in a car crash in Paris, France. The world was shocked. In the UK, people wept openly. They laid flowers outside Diana's home in London. Loved for her warm-hearted ways, she was called the "People's Princess" by Prime Minister Tony Blair when he spoke to the nation after the tragedy. His words struck a chord. At such a time, people wanted their Queen to show herself. Yet Elizabeth was still in Scotland, comforting her grandsons who had lost their mother, and shielding them from prying media eyes. But the public wanted to know why she was not in London and why the Palace flag had not been lowered to half-mast as a sign of mourning.

The Queen and Prince Philip view flowers left at Kensington Palace, Diana's London home.

Some of the criticism was personal, saying that Elizabeth seemed cold and out of touch, when many people wanted her to show she shared their sadness. True to herself as ever, Elizabeth saw the crisis through. She went back to London. She laid her own flowers and she spoke live on TV for the first time. After the overflow of feeling at Diana's funeral, she steadied the nation.

Chapter 12

Anchor for an age

The world continued to admire the Queen as a firm anchor in an unsafe world. She rarely tired and always showed total commitment to her role.

Queen Elizabeth welcomed in the year 2000 by singing "Auld Lang Syne" at an event at London's Millennium Dome. With the new millennium, Elizabeth knew her family must move with the times.

After the shocking terrorist attacks on 9/11 in the US in 2001 came further bombings in London in 2005. This meant extra security was needed for everyone. Armed guards were placed outside the Palace, with protection police guarding the Queen at all times.

Family sorrow came, too. In February 2002, Elizabeth's much-loved sister Margaret died and in March she lost her mother, aged 101. Of the York family living in Piccadilly all those years ago, Elizabeth was now the only one left.

In 2005, Prince Charles got married again. With his new wife, Camilla, he began taking on more of his mother's duties. However, though she was well past retirement age, Queen Elizabeth still kept up her busy routine.

For her Golden Jubilee in 2002, Elizabeth witnessed Buckingham Palace lit up by lasers. After 50 years as Queen, royal visits were now taken at a gentler pace. In 2006, she traveled to

The royal couple in 2002, the Queen's Golden Jubilee year.

Sharing the joke with President Bush at the White House in 2007.

Australia for the Commonwealth Games. The following year, she met with President George W. Bush in the US. In his welcome speech, Bush turned to wink at her—by accidentally giving the wrong date, he had suggested that the Queen was over 200 years old!

On her 80th birthday, Elizabeth invited 99 other people with the same birthday—April 21, 1926—to have lunch with her at the Palace. She told them that growing old means "we can give thanks for some wonderful memories and the excitement that each new day brings."

A very special day came in April 2011, when her grandson Prince William married Catherine (Kate) Middleton. Millions watched the royal wedding on TV, and the Queen gave the couple the titles of Duke and Duchess of Cambridge.

William and Kate on their wedding day, at Westminster Abbey, London.

William and Kate with their three children *(left to right)*: Louis, George, and Charlotte.

Soon Queen Elizabeth was to enjoy becoming great-grandmother to three more royal children— George, Charlotte, and Louis.

In 2011, the Queen made another historic trip—to the Republic of Ireland. The visit was a big step in improving relations between Britain and Ireland made worse by The Troubles in Northern Ireland. She wore green when she arrived in the "Emerald Isle," so called for its soft green landscape. For the state banquet, she chose a dress decorated with thousands of Irish shamrocks. Her speech at the dinner began with words in Irish Gaelic. In recalling past troubles, she said, "we can all see things which we would wish had been done differently …"

The Queen probably met more world leaders during her lifetime than anyone else. She held weekly meetings with her UK prime minister (15 in her reign), hearing their reports and offering advice. She had already met 11 American presidents when she welcomed President Barack Obama and his wife, Michelle, to the UK. On that

Barack and Michelle Obama were royal guests in 2011. The President praised the Queen's "extraordinary service."

occasion, as always, Philip was at her side to entertain the guests and was, at 90, as lively as ever. The Queen had a surprise gift for her husband to thank him for his lifelong support—the title Lord High Admiral, the top rank of the Royal Navy. Elizabeth knew how much he had missed the sea after giving up his career in the Navy when she became queen.

In 2012 came her Diamond Jubilee, marking 60 years as queen, and in the summer, the opening of the London Olympics.

QUEEN MEETS BOND

Queen Elizabeth sky-dived from a helicopter to open London's 2012 Olympic Games! That was how it looked to a TV audience of 900 million. At Buckingham Palace she had met secret agent James Bond (or the actor Daniel Craig). Together they rode by taxi to a helicopter that flew them to the Olympic stadium. Out jumped "the Queen" by parachute. The crowd gasped—then realized the jumper was in fact a stuntperson.

In September 2015, Elizabeth became the UK's longest-reigning monarch, breaking Queen Victoria's record of 63 years and 216 days. Yet she still moved with the times, using laptops and social media, even as the royal family faced further changes.

In 2018, Prince Harry married Meghan Markle, and they later chose to live outside the family circle. In 2020, speaking on TV, the Queen recalled her first radio broadcast in 1940, when families were separated by war, just as now they were parted by the covid pandemic. A year later, she felt deep personal loss when Prince Philip, her

husband of 73 years, died aged 99.

Her Platinum Jubilee in 2022 brought public celebration. Elizabeth lit the first in a chain of more than 3,000 beacons across the nation, took tea "virtually" with Paddington Bear, and on June 5, stood on the balcony at Buckingham Palace, cheered by a huge crowd. On September 6, she officially appointed the UK's new prime minister at Balmoral Castle in Scotland. Two days later, the world learned the sad news: Queen Elizabeth had died.

Charles is the third UK monarch of that name, and his wife Camilla is Queen Consort. With Charles' reign, new coins, notes, and stamps would carry the image of the king, replacing the head of Elizabeth.

Elizabeth's death marked the closing of a long chapter in history. Her eldest son and heir became king, as Charles III, with his wife Camilla as Queen Consort. King Charles, at 73, spoke warmly of Elizabeth as "a cherished sovereign and a much-loved mother." Two future kings were present at the funeral ceremonies—Elizabeth's grandson William and

her great-grandson
Prince George.

The state funeral
for the Queen began
with a lying-in-state
inside Westminster
Hall. There followed
a solemn procession,
and a funeral service in
Westminster Abbey attended by many heads of
state and government leaders. Her final journey
was to Windsor, where the Queen was laid to
rest in St. George's Chapel beside her husband,
father, mother, and sister. Her remarkable life
had reached its peaceful close.

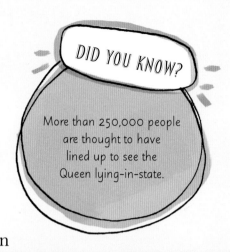

DID YOU KNOW?

More than 250,000 people
are thought to have
lined up to see the
Queen lying-in-state.

The Queen's coffin making its way through London from Buckingham Palace.

Elizabeth's family tree

Elizabeth,
the Queen Mother
1900–2002

Mother

Prince Philip,
Duke of Edinburgh
1921–2021

Husband

Queen
Elizabeth II
1926–2022

King Charles
III
1948–

Son

Anne,
Princess
Royal
1950–

Daughter

Andrew,
Duke of
York
1960–

Son

Edward,
Earl of
Wessex
1964–

Son

King
George V
1865–1936

Grandfather

Mary,
Queen Consort
1867–1953

Grandmother

King George VI
1895–1952

Father

Princess Margaret,
Countess of
Snowdon
1930–2002

Sister

Timeline

The future Queen Elizabeth is born to Albert and Elizabeth, Duke and Duchess of York.

King George V dies. Elizabeth's uncle becomes King Edward VIII. Elizabeth is now third in line to the throne.

Elizabeth's baby sister, Margaret, is born.

1926   1930   1936   1937   1944

King George V gives Elizabeth a Shetland pony named Peggy for her fourth birthday.

Edward VIII announces he is abdicating to marry Wallis Simpson.

Elizabeth's father, Albert, is crowned King George VI.

Elizabeth joins the ATS (Auxiliary Territorial Services), the women's branch of the British Army.

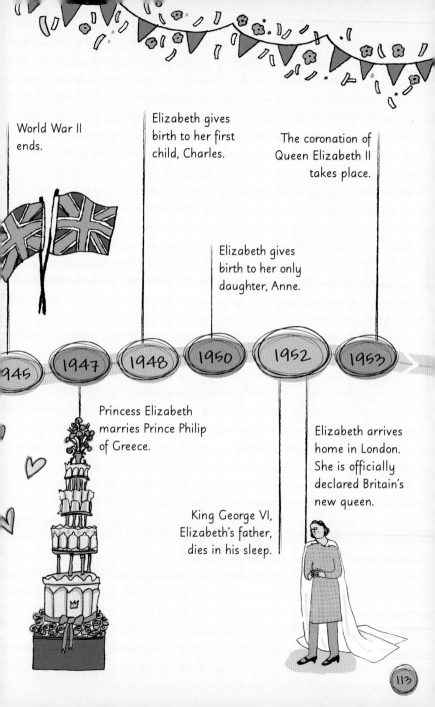

World War II ends.

Elizabeth gives birth to her first child, Charles.

The coronation of Queen Elizabeth II takes place.

Elizabeth gives birth to her only daughter, Anne.

1945   1947   1948   1950   1952   1953

Princess Elizabeth marries Prince Philip of Greece.

Elizabeth arrives home in London. She is officially declared Britain's new queen.

King George VI, Elizabeth's father, dies in his sleep.

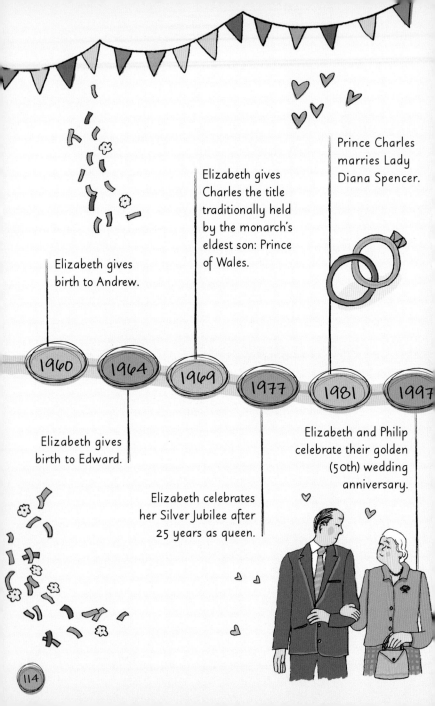

Elizabeth gives birth to Andrew.

Elizabeth gives Charles the title traditionally held by the monarch's eldest son: Prince of Wales.

Prince Charles marries Lady Diana Spencer.

1960   1964   1969   1977   1981   1997

Elizabeth gives birth to Edward.

Elizabeth celebrates her Silver Jubilee after 25 years as queen.

Elizabeth and Philip celebrate their golden (50th) wedding anniversary.

114

Queen Elizabeth celebrates her Golden Jubilee—50 years on the throne.

Elizabeth celebrates 60 years as queen—her Diamond Jubilee.

Queen Elizabeth makes a historic visit to the Republic of Ireland.

Elizabeth celebrates 70 years as queen, her Platinum Jubilee. Later that year, on September 8, she dies peacefully at Balmoral Castle, Scotland.

2002   2006   2011   2012   2015   2022

To celebrate her 80th birthday, the Queen invites 99 other people also born on April 21 to lunch at the palace.

Elizabeth becomes the UK's longest-reigning monarch, breaking Queen Victoria's record.

Quiz

1 How old was Queen Victoria, Elizabeth's great-great-grandmother, when she came to the throne?

2 What treat did Elizabeth choose for her fourth birthday breakfast?

3 Why did George V keep Sandringham's clocks half an hour fast?

4 What did Margaret say when she found out Elizabeth would be queen someday?

5 What did Elizabeth learn to do in the ATS?

6 Which Queen of the UK was Elizabeth and Philip's common relative?

7 Why did British people rush out to buy TVs in 1953?

Did you enjoy the book? Show us what you know!

 8 What title did Elizabeth give her son Charles in 1969?

 9 How many years as queen did Elizabeth celebrate on her Silver Jubilee in 1977?

 10 What was the name of the first Welsh corgi puppy to join the royal family?

 11 What did Tony Blair call Princess Diana?

 12 How many years of ruling did Queen Elizabeth celebrate on her Golden Jubilee in 2002?

Answers on page 128

Who's who?

Armstrong-Jones, Antony (Earl of Snowdon)
(1930–2017) society photographer and Margaret's husband from 1960 to 1978

Blair, Tony
(1953–) British prime minister from 1997 to 2007

Camilla, Queen Consort
(1947–) married Prince Charles in 2005

Catherine (Kate), Princess of Wales
(1982–) wife of Prince William

Charles III
(1948–) Elizabeth's eldest child; King from 2022

Churchill, Winston
(1874–1965) Prime Minister of the UK (1940–1945 and 1951–1955)

Crawford, Marion
(1909–1988) Elizabeth and Margaret's governess

Diana, Princess of Wales
(1961–1997) married to Prince Charles from 1981 to 1996

Edward VIII (later Duke of Windsor)
(1894–1972) Elizabeth's uncle; he gave up the throne

Elizabeth, the Queen Mother
(1900–2002) Queen Elizabeth's mother

George V
(1865–1936) King from 1910 to 1936

George VI
(1895–1952) Elizabeth's father, King from 1936 to 1952

Harry, Prince (Duke of Sussex)
(1984–) younger son of Charles and Diana

Knight, Clara
(1879–1946) nanny to Elizabeth

MacDonald, Margaret
(1904–1993), known as
"Bobo," nanny and friend
to Elizabeth

Mandela, Nelson
(1918–2013) President of South
Africa from 1994 to 1999

**Markle, Meghan
(Duchess of Sussex)**
(1981–) wife of Prince Harry

Mary, Queen Consort
(1867–1953) wife of
King George V

Obama, Barack
(1961–) President of the
United States from 2009
to 2017

Obama, Michelle
(1964–) First Lady of the
United States from 2009
to 2017

Reagan, Ronald
(1911–2004) President of
the United States from 1981
to 1989

Roosevelt, Eleanor
(1884–1962) First Lady of
the United States from 1933
to 1945

Roosevelt, Franklin D.
(1882–1945) President of
the United States from 1933
to 1945

Sarah, Duchess of York
(1959–) married to Prince
Andrew from 1986 to 1996

**Simpson, Wallis (Duchess
of Windsor)**
(1896–1986) Edward's wife
after he abdicated the throne

Thatcher, Margaret
(1925–2013) British prime
minister from 1979 to 1990

Townsend, Peter
(1914–1995) equerry to the
King, and the man Margaret
wanted to marry

Victoria
(1819–1901) Queen from
1837 to 1901

William, Prince of Wales
(1982–) elder son of Charles
and Diana

Wilson, Harold
(1916–1995) British prime
minister (1964–1970
and 1974–1976)

Glossary

abdicate
give up being king or queen

Apartheid
political system that used to exist in South Africa that used a system of separation based on race

auxiliary
extra help

Balmoral Castle
Scottish home of the British royal family

baptism
ceremony to mark a person joining the Christian Church

BBC
British Broadcasting Corporation: national broadcaster for the UK

blanks
fake bullets that sound like real bullets

Blitz, the
bombing attacks by German aircraft on cities in the UK during World War II

broadcast
sent out information using radio or television signals

Buckingham Palace
official London home of the British royal family

Caesarean section
operation to help a mother give birth; also called a C-section

Cenotaph
monument in London built to honor people who have died in war

christened
given a name at baptism as a sign of admission into the Christian Church

Commonwealth
group of nations that grew from the old British Empire

consort
wife or husband of a reigning monarch

coronation
ceremony to crown a new king or queen

crown jewels
scepter, crown, and other precious items used as symbols of royalty

empire
several regions or countries controlled by one person or country

engagement
social plan or event; also an agreement to marry

equerry
aide or assistant

European Union (EU)
group of European countries joined by close trading and political agreements

evacuated
moved out of a dangerous place and into a safer place; for example, in wartime

exhibition
public show of industry, art, or science

exile
having to live away from one's home country, usually for political reasons

general strike
when most workers in a country refuse to work

governess
woman hired to teach the children of a family

inquiry
investigation

investiture
ceremony in which the monarch honors someone

lady-in-waiting
assistant to a princess or queen

millennium
period of a thousand years

monarch
ruler of a kingdom or empire

nanny
someone paid to care for children and who sometimes lives with the family

pantomime
fun stage play for children, often put on at Christmas

paparazzi
photographers who chase after celebrities

RAF
Royal Air Force

ration
control the amount of something that people are allowed to have

regiment
large unit of soldiers, led by a colonel

Sandringham
country home of the British royal family

scepter
decorated rod held by a king or queen as a symbol of royalty

scuttling
moving fast with small steps

sovereign
king or queen or other royal ruler of a country

spellbound
so interested in something or someone that you give them all your attention

stuffy
old-fashioned and formal

transatlantic
crossing the Atlantic Ocean

Trooping the Colour
when soldiers parade with the colorful flags of their regiments in honor of the monarch's birthday

undiluted
pure

wary
not completely trusting

Windsor Castle
ancient fortress home of English kings and queens

Index

Acknowledgments

The author would like to thank: all those who worked in uniquely challenging circumstances to produce this book, with special thanks to our editor.

DK would like to thank: Caroline Hunt for proofreading; Maya Frank-Levine for the resource section; Helen Peters for the index; Roohi Sehgal and Radhika Haswani for editorial assistance.

The publisher would like to thank the following for their kind permission to reproduce their photographs:
(Key: a-above; b-below/bottom; c-center; f-far; l-left; r-right; t-top)

9 Alamy Stock Photo: Lebrecht Music & Arts (br). 10 Alamy Stock Photo: Photo 12 (tl). 13 Alamy Stock Photo: Trinity Mirror / Mirrorpix (b). 14 Alamy Stock Photo: North Wind Picture Archives (tr). 15 Alamy Stock Photo: Classic Image. 17 Getty Images: Universal History Archive / Universal Images Group (cra). 19 Alamy Stock Photo: History and Art Collection (tr). 21 Getty Images: Fox Photos (tl). 22 Alamy Stock Photo: Classic Image (br). Getty Images: (bl); Universal History Archive / Universal Images Group (t). 25 Getty Images: Paul Popper / Popperfoto (br). 27 Getty Images: Popperfoto (t). 28 Getty Images: Lisa Sheridan / Studio Lisa (bl). 29 Getty Images: Universal History Archive / Universal Images Group (t). 33 Alamy Stock Photo: Keystone Press (br). 35 Dreamstime.com: Andersastphoto (b). 36 Alamy Stock Photo: Everett Collection Inc (br). 37 Getty Images: Mondadori (t). 38 Alamy Stock Photo: GL Archive (br). 41 Getty Images: Reg Speller / Fox Photos (c). 44 Getty Images: Topical Press Agency (cb). 47 Getty Images: Stock Montage (cr). 49 Getty Images: Central Press / Hulton Archive. 51 Getty Images: Popperfoto (bl). 53 Getty Images: Popperfoto. 57 Getty Images: Keystone / Hulton Archive (b); The National Archives / SSPL (tr). 58 Dreamstime.com: Werdiam (cb). 59 Getty Images:

Evening Standard (tr). 62 Alamy Stock Photo: The Print Collector (br). 63 Dreamstime.com: Steve Allen (bl). 65 Getty Images: Bettmann (b). 67 Alamy Stock Photo: Shawshots. 69 Alamy Stock Photo: David Cole (br). 70 Alamy Stock Photo: Keystone Press (clb). Getty Images: STF / AFP (b). 71 TopFoto.co.uk: (t). 72 Alamy Stock Photo: Ajax News & Feature Service (ca). 73 Getty Images: Keystone-France / Gamma-Keystone (tr). 74 Alamy Stock Photo: The Print Collector (t). 77 Getty Images: Fox Photos / Hulton Archive (t). 81 Alamy Stock Photo: M&N (t). 83 Getty Images: David Levenson (t). 85 Getty Images: Tim Graham Photo Library (br). 87 Getty Images: Terry Fincher / Princess Diana (t); Tim Graham Photo Library (b). 88 Alamy Stock Photo: David Cooper (br). 92 Dreamstime.com: Markwaters (clb). Getty Images: Chip HIRES / Gamma-Rapho (tr). 95 Rex by Shutterstock: (t). 97 Getty Images: Lichfield Archive (br). 98 Getty Images: Martin H. Simon-Pool (tl). 99 Getty Images: Chris Jackson. 100 Getty Images: Max Mumby / Indigo (t). 101 Getty Images: Chris Jackson - WPA Pool (b). 105 Getty Images: Chris Jackson. 106 Alamy Stock Photo: Doug Peters / Empics (t). 108-109 Alamy Stock Photo: Hugo Philpott. 111 Getty Images: Bettmann (clb)

All other images © Dorling Kindersley

ANSWERS TO THE QUIZ ON PAGES 116–117

1. 18; 2. fish; 3. so no one would be late for meals; 4. "Poor you;" 5. Drive and repair army trucks; 6. Queen Victoria; 7. to watch Queen Elizabeth's coronation; 8. Prince of Wales; 9. 25; 10. Dookie; 11. the "People's Princess;" 12. 50